Small Talk

How to Talk to People, Start Conversations, Improve Your Charisma, Social Skills and Lessen Social Anxiety

2nd Edition: Updated & Expanded

ASTON SANDERSON

Copyright © 2017 Aston Sanderson
All rights reserved.

CONTENTS

1	Introduction	1
2	Mindset & Approach	3
3	Nerves & How to Calm Them	5
4	Good Listening is Your Greatest Ally	10
5	What to Say	14
6	Not All Questions are Created Equal	19
7	Feedback & Ending a Conversation	22
8	Conversation Starters	25
9	Body Language	29
10	Small Talk for Dating	33
11	Why You'll Make a Mistake & That's OK	38
	Conclusion	40
	Further Reading	41

CHAPTER 1

INTRODUCTION

Thank you for taking the time to download this book. You've taken the first step toward becoming an interesting conversationalist and someone that new people that you meet will remember.

Why Small Talk Matters

Meeting new people can be hard for anyone, but with these proven strategies and tips, you'll find yourself growing more confident and beginning to enjoy the challenge of meeting someone new and developing a real, personal connection with them.

In these chapters, you'll learn how to increase your social skills and lessen your social anxiety. We will take your through techniques of good listening, provide a list of conversation starters, address body language, and more.

At the completion of this guide, you will have all the tools you need to get out and meet new people immediately with greater ease and confidence.

Once again, thanks for downloading this small talk guide, and I hope you find it to be helpful.

Why Is Small Talk Important?

Humans are, in our very essence, social animals.

We seek approval from others, and feel most comfortable fitting in with our families, our peers, our culture and the world at large.

Being socially inept can mean being rejected, which evolution has taught us is a bad feeling we'd like to avoid. Societies have been based for thousands of years on people getting along, working together, building community, and marching together toward progress.

"Wow — all that, just from talking about the weather?" is what you might be thinking.

But it's true! We are social animals, and talking is our way of getting to know one another. Small talk is a way for people to break down their barriers and show each other through small conversation that the situation and the person they are talking to is safe. Only after establishing the tiniest bit of trust can we begin to form actual relationships through deeper conversation with those we don't know. Everyone you have met, perhaps for your family members, once started as an acquaintance you most likely had to engage in small talk.

We've all done it, but no matter how much experience we have, for anyone, meeting a stranger can be hard. But you don't need to hide away from fear of feeling nervous or having social anxiety.

Even for the most experienced, gregarious conversationalists, meeting new people always comes with the risk of rejection.

In these chapters you will learn how to conquer your fear, master your body language, find good topics to talk about and finally get out there and start meeting people with confidence.

CHAPTER TWO

Mindset & Approach

Like anything in life, the most important thing about small talk is the way you approach it.

All the strategies, tips, hacks and conversation starters won't make a difference if you're stuck in a negative pattern of thinking. Don't get stuck in a fixed mindset based in fear, self-doubt or irrationality.

What is a fixed mindset? A fixed mindset means you think that who you are at this moment is who you have always been and who you will always be.

You may think:

"I'm not good at meeting new people."

"I always say the wrong thing and make a bad first impression."

"Social skills are just not my thing."

"I'm happy just staying home; they won't miss me at the party."

But those are all fixed mindset phrases.

You should focus on a growth mindset. A growth mindset means that you realize and accept that things are constantly changing in your life, all around you, and in your skills and actions.

You may not be the best conversationalist today, but everyone can get some strategies (like you've done by buying this book), practice them, and become better over time.

So let's turn those fixed mindset phrases into growth mindset phrases:

"I'm not good at meeting new people" becomes *"I'm getting better at meeting new people."*

"I always say the wrong thing and make a bad first impression" becomes *"I am learning what to say around people, and improving the first impressions I make."*

"Social skills are just not my thing" becomes *"Social skills are an area of my life I have the capacity, ability and desire to improve."*

"I'm happy just staying home; they won't miss me at the party" becomes *"I am discovering new things about myself by getting out of my comfort zone, and I may be surprised how much fun I can have at a party."*

See how the "I am only this way," type of thoughts become "I am becoming better and constantly improving and working on it" thoughts?

So, even if you think you are not the most beautiful social butterfly out there, you can remember that (to use a well-worn metaphor), all butterflies were once caterpillars.

If you believe that you are bad at social situations, you have already sabotaged yourself.

Believe that you can get better, and you've already taken the first, and possibly most difficult, step.

In the next chapter, we'll look at how you can address your nerves and calm them.

CHAPTER THREE
Nerves & How to Calm Them

We cross the threshold into the party. We deliver the wine we brought, hug the host, smile, and excitedly catch up with her.

But then — the host has dozens of other guests to attend to. She disappears as the doorbell rings.

Now what do we do?

The party seems full of people who are frightening to approach — people who *may* not like us. It's certainly a possibility.

We imagine walking up to someone and starting a conversation, but we wonder, will they like us? What will they think of us? Facing rejection is tough, no matter how small it is. Even if someone we don't know at all rejects us, we wonder why and may go down a spiral in our head of thinking why and getting down on ourselves.

Facing all that overthinking, when a party is just supposed to be fun, can be hard!

So how can we overcome nerves?

Breathe

It sounds simple, but when we are nervous, our bodies can take over without us realizing it. We may start to sweat, our breathing becomes rapid and shallow, our thoughts race, and our stomach can feel upset.

But what caused this physical reaction? Just our thoughts. So it works in reverse, too. Calming our bodies can also help to calm our minds, just as our minds affect our bodies. This is called the mind-body connection, and it has more influence than you think.

So re-enter your body when you are feeling nervous in a social situation. Become aware that you are just standing in a room with people, not on the savannah about to be eaten by a lion, like your body's nerves are conditioned to respond through evolution. You are safe. Remember to breathe.

Focus on your breath, and your body will calm. Your heart rate will slow, your breathing will be more even, your stomach will settle, and your thoughts may stop racing.

If you can, count to five while breathing slowly in through your nose, filling your stomach, not your lungs. Feel the deep breath fully. Then, release the breath to the count of five as well, through your mouth. These deep breaths will calm your nervous system.

If your are a party, however, you can do these breaths under the radar instead of making a big scene about it in front of everyone! Take the opportunity to practice your breathing in the car before you go into the party, or while you are walking down the block. You can ask to use the bathroom straight away and then do some deep breathing in there. Don't be the weirdo standing in the corner huffing and puffing!

Remember That Your Reaction is Normal

The no. 1 fear of many people is public speaking, as it's so ingrained in our biology. As the comedian Jerry Seinfeld said,

> *"According to most studies, people's number one fear is public speaking. Number two is death. Death is number two. Does that sound right? This means to the average person, if you go to a funeral, you're better off in the casket than doing the eulogy."*

And even the most practiced public speakers still get nervous before going on stage, often experiencing the bodily symptoms we just discussed in the last section. Even if they don't feel nervous in their mind, physical reactions tend to be the same across people.

No matter how confident you are, you can still feel nervous.

So remember that you are not the only person at the party, or the meeting, or work event who is feeling nervous.

If you remember this, you won't feel so alone. It's OK to admit to yourself that you are scared. Just remember that a lot of other people are, too.

In fact, getting a bit of distance from our emotions and reactions can allow us to the space we need to acknowledge them but lessen their power over us. This is a technique from meditation called "labeling." When you label a feeling or emotion, it has less power over you, because you recognize that you are not the emotion, you are just experiencing the emotion, and it is temporary. So when you are feeling stressed, think to yourself:

- I am feeling stress
- I acknowledge that I am having thoughts of nervousness
- My body is reacting to this situation with nervousness

Even just the simple act of naming your emotions and feelings can allow you some relief from them.

Meet A Lot of New People

Another way to calm your nerves is to practice!

In psychology, when someone is afraid of spiders, a tactic used to help them get over that fear is called "systematic desensitization."

This means exposing the person over and over to spiders. First, it may just be a photo of spider. Then, it is larger photos of spiders. In the next step, the psychologist will hold a spider at a distance. Finally, the patient may be able, by him or herself, to hold the spider, and he or she has conquered the fear slowly, through these increased stages.

You can use the theory of systematic desensitization in your life as well, for meeting new people.

If you get used to meeting new people all the time, you will slowly become less frightened of it, just like the person with a fear of spiders. You can start slowly, by just making it your goal to make small talk with someone you already know, perhaps at a coworker at the office who you don't talk to much. Then, move on to a bigger goal, like making extra small talk with your coffee barista in the morning, or someone familiar but who you don't really know. Then move on to making small talk with a stranger to you, but maybe someone that a friend of yours knows. If you always get brunch with your friend Lucy on Sundays, ask Lucy to bring a friend of hers you've never met before along. There will not be as much social pressure, as Lucy will be there to facilitate conversation, but you also get the opportunity to practice small talk with a complete stranger, in more of a safe environment.

Keep increasing your goals each week, slowly, and soon enough you will find yourself feeling more confident in meeting new people.

So remember that at first, meeting new people will feel difficult and scary. But with each subsequent social situation, you will feel more and more comfortable.

Social Anxiety

We all suffer from some form of mild social anxiety. It is nerve-wracking to approach a stranger and face the fear of rejection. We also fear awkward silences, or that someone could be mean or rude to us.

But often, we area "catastrophizing" an event or situation in our head. If we feel the slightest bit nervous about something, we can imagine all the ways it will go wrong, visualize the worst-case scenario, and convince ourselves we need to get out of that situation, pronto.

But of course, the worst rarely transpires, especially in the way we see it in our minds. We worry no one at the party will like us and we will be laughed at. We worry we will completely forget the words to our work presentation speech, or to wear our pants to work that day, as the common nightmare goes. These mental crutches hold us back, however. Because our brains are naturally inclined to think of negatives rather than positives, we don't think of the *best case scenario*. But what if we did? We imagine that we connect really well with someone at the party, perhaps someone we can see again as a friend or potential dating partner. We can imagine that our work presentation goes so well that a coworker or our boss compliments us on it afterward (and that we remembered to wear our pants!)

If we don't attempt to exercise a bit of intentionality with regard to our imaginations, they can run wild and get away from us. So, a tactic you can use if you experience social phobia is to imagine all the good ways a scenario can go, and try to minimize all the negative things you imagine. Or, you can make an attempt to limit your imagination entirely, and try not to think about possible outcomes for the event, presentation, or date. After all, it hasn't transpired yet, and worrying does nothing to improve the future, it only ruins the present moment, as the saying goes.

Another strategy for social phobia, when it keeps us from getting out of the house in the first place, is to remember that you only need to attend the party for a half hour if you like. You can always leave. Sometimes, I have trouble pushing myself out of my comfort zone if the idea of an event is making me nervous, or I convince myself that I'd have more fun staying in. But I only need to remember that I can return home whenever I like, and then I know that I can push myself to go out for at least 30 minutes.

One final note about social anxiety: Though most of us probably suffer from a mild form or social shyness, if you suffer from diagnosed social anxiety, it is best to consult a trusted and licensed medical professional about steps you can take.

In the next chapter, we will discuss how *listening* is actually the most important part of *talking*.

CHAPTER FOUR

Good Listening is Your Greatest Ally

It may sound weird to say that the best way to improve your conversational and small talk skills is to *say nothing at all*.

But that's exactly what this chapter is about.

Often, when we are engaged in a conversation that puts us out of comfort zone, we focus so much on saying the right thing and our minds racing that we forget to ever listen to what the other person is saying.

This idea — that people are terrible at listening to each other — may be comforting in general, to realize that a lot of people you talk to may not even be listening to what you say, so what does it matter if you're not interesting? But on the other hand, what kind of world is that, if we all go around talking and talking and never listening to each other? We can all work to become better listeners and engage each other on a deeper level.

Being a good listener is *extremely hard*. But it's one of the best ways to increase your likeability and the ease with which you get along with other people.

And just like the actual talking part of the conversation, listening skills can get better with practice.

Here are three ways you can improve your listening:

Picture It

When you listen to someone else, it is easy to get wrapped up in thinking about your own experiences and how they relate. This a great strategy to converse with someone new, as shared experiences or having things in common is a great way to break down barriers.

But if the person begins sharing the details of their recent trip to the coast, and you immediately start imaging your most recent beach trip and thinking about what you can share about it, you are totally missing what the other person is saying.

So when the person you are conversing with talks about the sailing adventure they went on, try to follow along by imaging it in your head. Can you picture the boat they took? When they gloss over that it was a three-day trip, you now can picture them sleeping on the boat each night. But wait — sleeping on the boat, was that hard? You know how it feels to get motion sickness in a car.

Now you have a great follow-up question. Maybe they actually found it really peaceful to sleep on the boat, like being rocked to sleep. Maybe they kept having nightmares it was sinking. Either way, you have a very specific question that shows you were really listening. The best follow-up questions are pulled from these key details. If you instead were spacing out and thinking about your own beach trip, and then realized they were talking about sailing anyway, so maybe you shouldn't share your story about getting sunburned at the beach, then you may default to a boring, unrelated question, like, "So, what do you do for work?" It's then obvious to the other person that you weren't listening, and maybe they feel they weren't telling an interesting story, and your conversation is probably not going very well.

Instead, just listen! Really listening opens up limitless paths to go down in your conversation, and the only way to find those paths is to really listen for the details of someone's experience.

If you can imagine their story and experience yourself in your mind, you will probably ask yourself the same questions that person did while experiencing it.

So use your imagination to your advantage! Keep your brain busy focusing on the pictured experiences of the other person, instead of your own experience and what you will say about it.

Give Your Full Attention

It may sound obvious, but don't get distracted. Resist the urge to pull out your smartphone, even if it's just to look something up to share with the person, because your brain will immediately jump to thinking about all the notifications from social media or your unread emails you can see.

So remain fully engaged and present with the person you are speaking to.

Keep eye contact, and don't let your gaze wander around the party, event or restaurant, wherever you may be. This body language signals that you are bored or looking for an out of the conversation, so remain focused. We'll talk more about body language in another chapter, but for now, just know that if you are giving your mental attention to a person, your body will show as much. It's easier to actually give your attention, rather than trying to fake it by appearing interested but really zoning out.

Giving someone your full attention, especially in the distractions-on-steroids world we live in with all of our gadgets and the whole of human knowledge at our fingertips, is one of the most respectful and generous things you can do. Wouldn't it be lovely for someone to just listen to you, fully and presently, without checking their email?

If you give the people you know (and those you have only just met) your full, undivided attention, you may find you start to receive the same in return more often, too.

Imagine You'll Tell Someone Later

One of the best tricks for comprehending something and remembering it is thinking of explaining it to someone else.

This is a strategy that students can use for tests, but it's also a mind frame you can use when listening to someone else speak. We recall information better when we process it in our own minds and have to repeat the information back.

If you imagine you will tell someone later about the conversation, you will be more likely to pay attention and remember the important parts.

In the next chapter, we will move on from listening to, yes, finally, the actual *talking* part of small talk!

CHAPTER FIVE
What To Say

Ugh, not the weather again!

Small talk gets a bad rap. Many people don't have particularly fascinating or important opinions or observations about the weather, and they don't want to hear anyone else's. They don't care about the local sports team. They don't want to talk about where they work, and for how long, again.

But remember that small talk plays an important social function in our society. This seemingly meaningless banter provides a way for us to get to know each other, and is a way for us to engage with each other that is non-threatening. Have you ever been having a bad day, and just the act of a cashier mentioning that the feel-better ice cream you bought yourself is their favorite flavor, too, made you feel better already? Connecting with others, even through such small, surface-level interactions, is extremely important to us social animals.

Even if it just makes you feel a tad better, interacting with people can help you feel not so wrapped up in your own thoughts, even if it is just "small" talk.

Small talk provides a low barrier of entry so we can all approach and talk to each other. If you walked up to strangers and asked them, "What is the most important memory from childhood?" you'd be pretty off-putting, to say the least.

But this is a question we'd feel comfortable discussing with best friends, our partners, or close family. At one time, each of those people was a stranger, too. And that wasn't the first thing we said to them.

So realize that anyone you speak to could become one of your close friends. It just doesn't happen overnight, or in the span on one conversation. Be patient, and make yourself and them comfortable at first by sticking to easy topics.

It can still be fun to talk about topics that aren't threatening or very deep.

You can try:

> *Travel*
> *The host you both know*
> *Movies or TV you find you have in common*
> *The city you live in*
> *What you are doing for a coming holiday, or what you did for one that just passed*

People love to talk about themselves, so if you can get someone to talk about themselves, instead of the weather, it will probably already be much more engaging for both of you.

Small talk doesn't have to be small! We'll show you how to have better small talk conversations, ones that actually lead to getting to know someone, in the next chapter.

But first, here are some ideas of what to say when engaged in small talk:

Find Common Ground

The first strategy for what to say in small talk is finding common ground. Any topic will be easier to discuss when both people in the conversation have something to add about it.

The most obvious immediate thing you both have in common, unless you're talking on the phone, is your immediate surroundings. So you can comment on the immediate situation.

If you are at a party and mention the good music, or the great snack table, or how great the turnout is, and the stranger you mention it to says more than one word, they are saying it's OK to engage them in conversation. This is a great way to take something you have in common to test the waters with someone.

Maybe you both hate the current song that's playing, or maybe you both love it.

Even if it's a stranger in the elevator, maybe you both just stepped inside from the rain, and the city's weather is obviously something you have in common. You can say something like "I hope this wet pattern we've been having stops soon," or "I can't remember if my windows are open at home, have you ever done that?"

Just say something innocuous and see where it takes you.

Following off of the common ground strategy, if you come across something you both have in common, more than the immediate situation or party you find yourselves at, make sure to explore that topic as much as you can! Maybe you both grew up playing soccer every summer. Maybe your grandmas are both from Southern California. Maybe you both love dogs!

It could be anything, but sharing a common quality or passion with someone new instantly ingratiates us to them. Especially if you both find a topic that is not common, like that you both participate in stamp collecting or Brazilian jiu-jitsu, you will really connect with someone who shares a unique passion of yours. We tend to get excited when we find someone who shares our particular brand of weird, whatever yours is!

Give Compliments & Information

The next strategy for what to say in small talks is to be *giving*. When you offer something to another person, the inherent value we place as a species on reciprocity means they'll want to give something back to you. Reciprocity is a pretty large concept, but for the purposes of small talk, it just means that offering something, like information about yourself, or a compliment, makes it easier for the other person to want to share something about themselves, as well.

First, let's tackle compliments.

Everyone loves receiving a compliment. Don't go overboard, but you can comment on something small and simple. Something like, "I love your shirt" is enough to get started chatting to someone new.

Of course, be aware that compliments can also easily come off as a little too weird or forward, especially as a man complimenting a woman. Don't get too personal with physical compliments, and stick to things people are wearing or carrying instead of commenting on their hair or body.

Next, let's look at giving something besides compliments: Information.
Conversing is all about sharing. If you don't share, the other person will find it more difficult to bounce back to you in the conversation if you don't give them anything to go on.

If they ask you where you went to college, instead of just saying, "Iowa," you can say, "Iowa, it was a very small town, which I loved, because I grew up in a big city."

That's revealing something about yourself — that you grew up in a city but also enjoy living in a small town.

You could follow it up with, "Do you prefer the city? Have you spent any time in the country?" and now you have a conversation flowing!

If the person you're talking to says (like our previous tip of commenting on the surroundings) something as small as, "Have you tried the popcorn at the snack table? It's so good."

Instead of just saying, "Yes, it's good." Or "No, I haven't," you can add, "Popcorn is basically the only reason I go to the movies, I've seen a lot of mediocre movies just to eat popcorn because movie theater popcorn is the best."

Now that person can agree or disagree with you, or ask you about a recent movie you've seen. They have a lot of options, since you've revealed something about yourself rather than just a "yes" or "no" answer.
The more you put forth, the more you should get in return. Of course, don't go on a 20-minute diatribe about your personal problems, but be willing to open up a bit, even if it feels unnatural.

STAY POSITIVE & LIGHT

Going off of the idea of not getting *too* personal right away, keep the conversation positive and light to begin with.

It's best not to start complaining or talking about something you don't like immediately after meeting someone new. No one likes to be around someone else who is super negative!

Also avoid the topics of health, religion and politics. These can be personal and controversial. Even if you think someone will probably agree with you on these topics, you can never be sure, and never "judge a book by its cover." Even if someone holds the same beliefs as you, talking about these heated topics can quickly become an intense conversation, and not in a good way.

If the topic is heading toward something in one of these areas, you can try to gently steer it away.

If you are talking about (of course!) the weather, and the other person mentions the crazy storm that happens on election day, and asks you whether you went out in the storm to vote, you can say steer the conversation away from its political implications and bring up a new topic. By bringing up a new topic instead of re-directing just to the weather aspect of their comment, you help avoid giving the other person an opportunity to bring up politics again.

Maybe say something like, "Oh yeah, I was out in that storm, I was worried about my dog all day! When I got home I couldn't find him, but eventually I found him hiding in the shower!"

Now you can safely talk about pets or dogs or fear of storms.

If the person is insistent about starting a political discussion, it may be best to move on. We'll give you strategies for exiting conversations in future chapters in this guide. But first, in the next chapter we will talk about keeping conversation flowing, by asking questions.

CHAPTER SIX

Not All Questions Are Created Equal

Questions, questions, questions!

Behind good listening, asking good follow-up questions is probably the most important part of mastering conversation and leveling up your small talk game.

So what makes a good question? Let's find out:

Good Questions are Open-Ended

Just like the advice to not answer questions with just a simple "yes" or "no," you can aim to ask questions that allow for more nuanced answers than these two words, as well, to encourage the other person to expand their answers. Questions that can be answered with a simple "yes" or "no" can be a conversation killer.
ou will get longer responses.

Remember the questions words:

How
What
Who
When
Where
Why

As you are getting to know someone in your conversation and feeling more comfortable, breaking out "why" is a great strategy to use to probe a bit deeper.

If someone mentions that Bucelli's is their new favorite restaurant in town, you can ask them why, and then they have a chance to share more about something they are excited about and feel very positively toward. Sometimes people are caught off-guard by "why" questions, because as we go about our lives, we rarely ask people why they think or do something. We just accept what is.

They may have to think for a minute, but then maybe they will say something like, "Bucelli's ravioli tastes just like my grandma used to make. She actually grew up in Italy. She taught me so many bad Italian words when I was a kid."

Their grandma sounds like a fabulous cook and spunky lady, what a great topic to ask more about!

Good Questions are Superlative

Good questions are also superlative. "Superlative" refers to the extremes of something: The best, the most, the least, the craziest, or someone's favorite.

When you ask a follow-up question, asking a superlative is a good way to have someone talk about something that they find engaging.

If someone mentions that they've been living in the same neighborhood for 10 years, you can ask them what the best thing about living there is, or their favorite thing about it. Clearly, they've stayed a while!

If someone mentions that they've worked in HR for years, you can ask what the craziest way someone quit a job was.

If someone loves traveling to Las Vegas, what's the biggest winning they've ever witnessed at the casino? The biggest loss? (But maybe not their own, that's a bit personal. For instance. "Have you ever seen someone win more than $10,000 at once, or set the slot machine off on one of those crazy ringing frenzies?")

Asking superlative questions makes for an easy way to open someone up about their most memorable experiences. Sometimes, I find that when someone asks me a superlative question, it sometimes is something I haven't thought about before. That makes that person a lot more memorable to me, as the conversation experience they provided was unique, interesting, engaging and new.

Don't Interrogate

Remember, don't let the other person do all the talking!

If you are feeling nervous, you may be inclined to share less instead of more. But then you give you conversational partner less to work with and ask you follow-up questions about.

So don't only ask questions, and don't ask a ton in rapid succession if you are not getting good responses back. This may be a sign that they are not interested in being asked so many questions about the topic you are inquiring about.

So also share about yourself for a bit, and feel comfortable doing it. If someone is sharing details about themselves with you, you should do the same as a courtesy with them.

Conversation is like a tennis match or a game of catch: You hit the ball back and forth, and each person should be contributing about equally. If someone is talking at you, this won't be a pleasant conversation experience, like getting tennis balls repeatedly hit at you when you're not even holding a racquet, or getting a ball thrown at you without a mitt. We will give you tips for exiting conversations like this in the next chapter.

CHAPTER SEVEN

Feedback & Ending a Conversation

Being good at small talk is not only about knowing how to talk and listen well. It's also about knowing how to end small talk conversations.

Sometimes, it is just the natural end to a good conversation and meeting someone new. However, sometimes we meet someone we'd rather not spend time conversing with (someone who brings up controversial topics, talks *at* us instead of to us, or in some way makes us uncomfortable). Don't feel badly about leaving conversations like this. I trust you to know the difference between a conversation that's not great because one or two of the people involved lack the knowledge of how to make good conversation but are nice people with good intentions, and a conversation that is uncomfortable because one person does not have good intentions or is just a blowhard or jerk.

In this chapter, we will look at how to end conversations gracefully, whether you can tell your conversation partner wants to leave, or you would like to end a conversation.

Signaling the End of a Conversation

First, let's look at how to notice if your conversation partner is using coded social cues to exit a conversation. They may try to let you know in a subtle way, as most people do when engaged in small talk.

Before we look at that, though, don't feel bad when someone is finished having a conversation with you. You are not going to be the new best friend and Most Interesting Person everyone has ever met, and that's true for everyone at all times.

Having a fabulous connection with someone the first time you meet them is rare, and you should appreciate it when it happens. But in a lot of cases, friendships or even acquaintances are built up over time through repeated meeting, shared experience, and many conversations, not just one or two.

Someone leaving a conversation doesn't mean that it was bad. Maybe the other person is in a hurry or needs to speak to someone else at the work function to ensure they get that promotion they were hoping for. Maybe they want to catch up with someone they haven't seen in months who is also at the party. You don't know the reason someone is done talking to you, but it often is not just that you are not worth talking to.

Here are some cues to look for that someone is ready to end a conversation:

>*They are not making eye contact, but constantly looking around*
>
>*They say "It was nice to meet you" or "It was nice talking to you," signaling that the conversation is over*
>
>*Their body language is "closed." This could be crossed arms, or their body pointing away from you and the conversation*
>
>*They mention another friend at the party and that they'd like to introduce the two of you, and the first person will probably not join that conversation*

You can also use any of these tactics on your own to exit a conversation.

How to Leave a Conversation

It's also nice to give someone an out of a conversation. If you have only been talking to that person for a long time at an event with a lot of people, you both should meet more than each other. You can say something like:

>*"Well, I'm sure you have a lot of other people to catch up with"*
>
>*"It's been so great talking to you, but I'm going to mingle a bit"*

"It's been great to talk to you, but I think I should meet a few of our host's other friends, too"

If you need to be a bit more forceful (like with that jerk blowhard), you can use "I need" statements. It is in our psychology to respect the things people say they "need," even if it is just a "want" in reality. You can say you need things like:

"Excuse me, I need to use the bathroom."

"I need to refill my drink. It was nice talking to you."

"I need to make a phone call, excuse me."

Like all things in life, even good conversations must come to an end. Don't feel bad about it, as that just means it is time to practice small talk with someone new. In the next chapter, we will discuss some phrases you can use as conversation starters when you meet new people.

CHAPTER EIGHT

Conversation Starters

At a loss for topics to talk about, ways to approach someone, or how to keep the conversation going after it's stalled a bit? In this chapter, we will add on a few tips about starting conversations and provide a list of good questions to spark interesting conversation.

Tip: Remember Names

It is incredibly important to remember peoples' names.

Many books about winning friends or getting people to like you suggest using a person's name as often as possible when talking to them. However, this "trick" has been around as advice for about 80 years, and it has been given as advice in the realm of sales. So I actually would advise against this strategy. We're so used to salespeople and telemarketers doing this to us so often, it tends to feel very salesy, off-putting, and fake.

However, I highly recommend remembering someone's name and using it once or twice in the conversation, usually at least when you say, "Well, it was nice talking to you, Jen" and leave a conversation.

When we meet someone new, we're getting so much sensory input and so wrapped up in how we're coming across and acting as well that the opportunity to actually hear and remember their name slips right by us. We worry about our handshake and grip (or whether we'll shake hands at all, as in some informal settings it is no longer customary to), how we'll introduce ourselves, what the person looks like, what we look like, how much eye contact to make, and on and on.

How often have you met someone and realized less than 5 seconds later that you have absolutely no idea what his or her name is? What you can do in this situation is be more mindful when you are meeting a new person, and really focus on their name, instead of all the other sensory stuff we get wrapped up in.

People are so bad at remembering names, that if you remember someone else's, they will feel really good and special.

If you forget their name still, you can politely ask with something like, "By the way, I'm so bad at names, I'm sorry, but what is your name again?"

They will probably be flattered that you even ask, as most people just try to avoid the topic of names once the initial introduction is over!

Prepare Beforehand

Another tip for beginning conversations is to prepare beforehand, if you know you are going into a situation where small talk will be made.

On your drive over to a barbecue, think of at least two or three conversation starters to bring up if a conversation begins to stall.

Scan a newspaper before you leave the house to see if there is a big news story you can talk about. (Though once again, avoid politics, religion or controversy.) Think of what movies recently came out and if you have any interesting information about them, like reviews or awards, even if you haven't seen them.

When there is silence in a conversation, you may immediately assume it's an "awkward silence." Do not have this mindset, however.

A period of silence will always feel much longer than it actually is, so don't feel stressed about how long the break in conversation is.

Also, the silence is just that: A break. Think of it as a transition in the conversation to a new topic. Perhaps you have naturally exhausted the things both of you have to say about the current topic, and you can now move on to something new. Or, perhaps you feel the conversation is finished and this is a good time to use one of your exit strategies from the last chapter.

Let's move on to a list of conversation starters you can use.

A List of Conversation Starters

Use the below questions to keep a conversation flowing once it has stalled or slowed, or to begin a new conversation.

Have you always done this [profession], or have you worked as anything else?

If you could fly anywhere in the world at no cost tomorrow, where would you go?

What was the best job you had growing up?

What's the best advice you've ever gotten?

What's the strangest compliment someone has given to you?

Do you have a book, movie or TV show that you love, but everyone else hates? What about something everyone else loves, but you hate?

If you could only eat one food for the rest of your life, what would you choose?

Does your family have any recipes that have been passed down for generations, or that are secret?

What was the last travel experience you had?

What's your favorite thing to do on the weekends?

Have you ever lived anywhere else? How is this place different?

Do you have a hidden talent, or a surprising hobby?

What's your favorite app on your phone?

Have you read any good books recently?

Have you ever had a boss who asked you to do something crazy?

What's your favorite unknown restaurant?

If you could have any superpower, what would it be?

What would you teach a college course on, if you could?

If you could have any animal as a pet, what one would you choose?

Did you catch up on the news today?

CHAPTER NINE

Body Language

We say a lot with our bodies, and we read a lot about how other people are feeling based on their body language and facial expressions, even if we don't realize we are all constantly communicating with this secret language.

So you need to make sure that your body language is saying what you want it to. Your body will probably naturally show how you are feeling, so if you are interested in speaking to someone, you will show it.

However, if you are not really interested in speaking to someone, or you are feeling nervous, your body may be sending the wrong signals to the other person.

In this chapter, we'll take a look at some body language signs, and you will learn how to read the body language of someone else, as well.

Your Body Language

When you are trying to communicate friendly body language, your body should generally be "open." That means no crossed arms, crossed legs if you are sitting, or turning your body angled away from the person you are talking to.

Other tips:

> *Smile and appear friendly*
>
> *Make eye contact but do not stare*

Stand a comfortable distance away from someone, not too close, nor sitting too close if on a couch

Avoid using your phone during the conversation

Avoid touching your face or hair excessively or do other nervous habits like picking at your nails or fidgeting

Don't tap your foot, as it could appear that you are impatient to leave the conversation

Don't chew gum

Relax your shoulders

Don't hold your drink or anything in front of your chest, as this can communicate that you feel guarded

It is also helpful to mimic the body language of the other person. Obviously not in the way we did this as kids to annoy our siblings ("Mom! She's copying me!) but this is a natural tactic we use unconsciously when we are getting along well with someone. If you become more aware of your body, you may notice yourself doing this unconsciously.

For example, you both may be nodding, or leaning in slightly, or moving your hands in the same way, or holding your drinks the same way.

Don't, however, overdo body language. In general, refraining from large movements or small tics will make the conversation and what you are communicating with your body flow more smoothly.

Above all else, a friendly, genuine smile can usually be worth more than any undesirable body language you may be displaying. So remember to relax and smile!

Reading Body Language

When you are speaking to another person, pay attention to their facial expressions, and this will communicate a lot that the person may not be expressing through their words directly.

Also be aware of how the other person is standing, and their posture and the way they hold their head.

For example, all the tips we gave you in the last section, be aware if someone else is putting off these body signals. They could just be nervous, but they may also be communicating that they are not that into the discussion you are having.

Here are a few things to keep in mind when reading body language:

A genuine smile will create wrinkles or creases next to the eyes; fake smiles involve the lips only

If someone is mimicking your body language, it means they like you and the conversation is going well

Someone may be lying if they hold eye contact for an extended period of time

Raised eyebrows or pursed lips can mean that the person is experiencing discomfort

A tight jaw means the person is stressed out

Crossed arms or legs are "closed" body position that may mean the person is not that open to your ideas or the conversation

An excessive amount of head nodding may mean the person is worried about getting your approval

Notice where the person's feet and legs are pointing. If it is away from you, they may be signaling they want to escape the conversation

Excessive blinking or facial movements can indicate anxiety

If someone looks at the floor a lot, they are probably shy or embarrassed

Normal eye contact is meeting the eyes and holding eye contact about 80% of the time, and usually not for more than 7 seconds

Leaning in towards you means the person is interested in the conversation (or maybe that the party is very loud!)

The last point that should be made about body language is that it can vary a bit from person to person, so don't automatically give up on a conversation if someone is crossing their arms, or think you have a new best friend if someone is leaning in to the conversation. Use body language cues in tandem with other context and what you know about small talk to assess how things are going.

That's just a brief intro to body language, as we could spend books explaining all its finer points. In the next chapter, we will look at small talk for dating. If you are in a committed relationships or don't have interest in dating, you may find this chapter interesting and helpful in a general sense of turning small talk into deeper talk.

CHAPTER TEN

SMALL TALK FOR DATING OR: TURNING SMALL TALK INTO DEEP TALK

When we start with small talk, we often want to make the conversation go a little deeper. Some people really hate talking about the weather (I'm not one of them; I find it endlessly fascinating), or some people hate talking about their job. No matter your feelings about small talk, the ability to turn a small talk conversation into something more, wether that's on a date or just making a new friend, is the key to lasting connections with people.

In this chapter, we'll look at a few ways to turn small talk conversations into deeper-level conversations.

STORIES ARE BETTER THAN FACTS

If your date conversation gets stuck in small talk, you may never find out if you really like the person and want to see him or her again. You want to get to a deeper level of talk and figure out if this relationships could work out.

The thing, is you don't need to put a lot of pressure on the first date to figure our if they want kids, want to settle down in the same city, or how much debt they have. Those thing can wait! For the first few dates, just try to assess if you enjoy each other's company and conversation.

Still, you don't want to talk about the local sports team the whole time. So some of the strategies we talked about in this book for using at a meeting, conference, or party can be deepened and expanded upon to make "small talk" into "deep talk."

First, let's talk about storytelling. Storytelling is extremely important to humans, and it is what we'll find most engaging in a conversation, instead of a straight exchange of facts.

So on your date, don't just exchange facts, but be more interesting by telling stories.

For example, as a response to the question, "What do you do," you can offer a story or detail, instead of only your job title and company name. Instead of saying "I'm a teacher for 4th grade," you can say, "I'm a 4th grade teacher, and one of my favorite parts of my job is seeing kids figure out new things and get excited about them. I had a girl who said she'd never painted before our art lesson last week, and now she is bringing me paintings she is doing at home." That's a great, short story that opens the window to talk about something you're passionate about — seeing kids discover new passions — while avoiding the boring parts of your job, like how much you hate grading or the long hours.

Storytelling is immediately more engaging than a simple statement of fact.

Here are a few engaging first date questions to ask:

> *What's a big influence in your life right now?*
> *Who has been your best teacher or professor in your life?*
> *What should I know about you that I may not think to ask about?*
> *What would your ideal Saturday look like?*
> *What makes you laugh a lot?*
> *What's your biggest goal you're working toward right now?*
> *What's the worst thing about dating?*
> *Any pet peeves I should know about?*
> *What were you like as a child?*
> *What's you favorite place in the whole world?*

And one last tip: Doing something engaging, like a cooking class or a hike, for a date will bring you closer together than grabbing a drink or eating a meal. There will be less silence to fill, and you'll have the experience to talk about as well to get to know each other. This may help the conversation flow more easily.

S<small>TAY</small> O<small>PEN</small> M<small>INDED</small>

One of the way humans make sense of the world is by putting things into boxes, labels and categories. If we couldn't do this, the world would be frighteningly complex (even more so than it is already!) We have pigeons, eagles, parrots and crows, but we know these are all types of birds, so they go in the bird category. This is helpful for us to understand what to expect when we encounter a bird we haven't seen before.

Sometimes though, these labels can be too simple, and they can keep us from discovering new things or being open minded. This is especially true in dating, when we're trying to assess whether this stranger is the kind of person we like and want to hang out with, the kind of person we could possibly fall in love with, the kind of person we're attracted to or not, or the kind of person who could end up hurting us.

That's a lot to figure out and a lot of pressure, and sometimes it can make us feel vulnerable. So we try to answer these questions quickly, with irrelevant identifiers like what color hair someone has, what they do for work, where they are from, etc.

If everyone we've met from California has been kind of a jerk, and we learn our date grew up in California, it is a shorthand mental strategy to put them in your Cali-jerk box and label. If they are a corporate lawyer or a professional musician, we have boxes and labels for these people as well. But all these boxes just serve to keep us from possibly really connecting with someone we haven't imagined ourselves connecting with before.

How does this relate to the small talk on your date? Try to collect more information about passions and what's important to a person than what they do for a living, where they went to school, or another question that might be a "box" question.

Instead of asking someone what they do for a living, ask them, "What's your favorite part of your daily routine?" or "What do you care about at the moment?"

These questions leave a lot of room for the other person to go very deep with their answers, or stay a bit more surface-level but still engage in a way they might not have if you just asked about work.

It is only by going a bit deeper than our boxes, though it can be uncomfortable, that we can truly get to know someone, and not just their labels.

Online Dating & Chat

A chapter about small talk in dating would be incomplete in this day and age without acknowledgment of how much of our small talk happens in chat.

No matter what kind of dating website or app you are using, there is bound to be a little bit of text chat before meeting up in person. I do recommend, however, that you move the chatting offline as soon as possible. There is so much we can learn about a person through a live meeting that we absolutely cannot know from text chat. When we talk in person, we have the added context of body language, voice inflection and tone, facial expressions, and immediate conversation, versus text responses that can be mulled over for the perfect witty response for hours.

And you may feel turned off by the way someone text chats, but everyone has a different approach to the unwritten etiquette rules of messaging online. So don't judge someone by the *way* they chat (judging them by the content of their chat is OK, if they are rude, etc.). Just accept that you don't really know what someone is like until you meet in person. Some people are just bad at texting, and may come off as robotic when they don't intend to.

But when you are involved in text chat, it's best to use the same principles that apply to in-person small talk.

Use the person's name, and ask them something about themselves they have mentioned in their profile or on linked social media accounts. Did they just attend a concert you heard was really amazing? Do they say they love animals? Did they recently go on an exotic trip? Asking something other than, "How are you?" or "What's up?" shows that you care enough to take a few minutes to learn something about a person instead of using a formulaic response. You may be surprised how many people don't take this simple step, and how much genuine niceness can stand out in online dating.

Small talk, once again, is the way we judge whether or not someone is "safe" to talk to, and unfortunately, can be a barrier to entry to deeper conversations. That doesn't mean it has to be boring, though! Use the techniques from this book, and you'll find yourself easily segueing from small talk to more interesting and revealing conversations, whether that is in your dating life or another area.

In the next chapter, we'll talk about recovering from social faux pas.

CHAPTER ELEVEN

Why You'll Make a Mistake & Why It Doesn't Matter

In this chapter, we will make one last note about small talk, now that you are becoming an expert! So here goes:

None of us is perfect. Even the greatest communicators, most gregarious people and biggest and most beautifully-winged social butterflies stumbles sometimes in a social situation. Maybe your conversation partner isn't making it easy for you and you have to do all the work. Maybe you had a bad day at the office and your mind is still at work. Maybe you are just having an off day or misjudged a joke that you thought would be funny. That's all totally OK!

We all make mistakes, and rest assured that everyone thinks about themselves a lot more than they ever think about you. Try to think of your most embarrassing moment from grade school or middle school. You can remember it pretty vividly, can't you? Did it happen in front of a lot of people? How many of your classmates do you think remember it today? Can you think of embarrassing moments of others you witnessed in school? Probably not as many as you can think of for yourself.

So remember to relax, it will all be **OK**. It feels overwhelming and terrible in the moment, but no one will remember your embarrassing social faux pas.

Another thing to remember about social skills is that they are learned. No one is born a social communicator. We all have to grow up and learn language and the ways people interact in our specific culture. If being gregarious and popular were innate, people would be revered across cultures. But it can be hard to talk to someone who doesn't share the same social rules and conversation markers from another country.

Some people are predisposed to liking social interaction more, or have had more experience or are more naturally inclined to it. But these are just social clues that can be learned, so you can learn them to. Everyone thinks they are worse at small talk than they are.

Your social skills are a muscle, and just like when you are weight training, you need to stretch them, work them, and keep stretching and working them and challenging them to grow those muscles. Right now, you may feel like you are lifting very little socially, with our weight lifting metaphor. Maybe you can only lift the bar. But with practice, you will be able to add a bit more weight, and then a bit more.

Weight training has a strategy of "training to failure," which means lifting until your body physically cannot do it anymore. Your body "fails" at the task. So each time you make a social faux-pas, you are training your social skills to failure, and therefore getting stronger.

After you go through these strategies and start to learn more about social skills, you will definitely make some missteps. And that's, once again, totally OK! It just means you are improving. As long as you learn from the situation, realize what you could have done better, and then move on, you are doing wonderfully.

Your social skill and small talk muscles are growing with each interaction, and especially those that you feel you didn't totally crush. Don't freak out and go into a downward spiral thinking that you are bad at small talk. You are growing, little caterpillar and future social butterfly, and that's what important.

In the last chapter of our small book on small talk, we'll summarize the important points we learned about socializing.

CONCLUSION

It's time to use what you have learned in this small talk guide. I hope that you've gained strategies you can use right now to improve your social skills and lessen social anxiety.

Remember, you can get out there today and use what you've learned. Remember these general tips:

> *Be confident and have a growth mindset*
>
> *Accept that you will feel nervous and that is normal*
>
> *Use the surroundings to start conversations*
>
> *Ask open-ended questions*
>
> *Share about yourself; don't give short answers*
>
> *Have friendly and open body language*
>
> *Avoid controversial topics*
>
> *Let the other person politely end the conversation; or do it yourself*
>
> *Remember that when you feel you made a social flub, it means you are working your conversation muscles and getting better!*

If you enjoyed this book, please take the time to leave me a review on Amazon. I appreciate your honest feedback, and it really helps me to continue producing high quality books.

Simply go to the book's Amazon page, or use link to go straight to your reviews page (you need to be signed in to your Amazon account): http://bit.ly/smalltalkreview Thank you!

FURTHER READING

Like what you read? Read two more books by author Aston Sanderson.

Have racing thoughts, a lot of negative self-talk, or worry and stress a lot? Learn strategies to change the way your thought patterns run and get your inner monologue to work *for* instead of against you.

Buy "Self Talk" at bit.ly/selftalkbook

"Self Talk: How to Train Your Brain to Turn Negative Thinking into Positive Thinking & Practice Self Love"

As a new dad, author Aston Sanderson has also written a book on how to choose a baby name the stress-free way, with a list of 3,000 baby names. Buy "The Stress Free Baby Names" book here: bit.ly/babynamesbook

"The Stress-Free Baby Names Book: How to Choose the Perfect Baby Name with Confidence, Clarity and Calm"

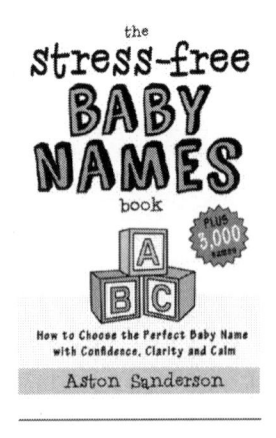

What do you want to learn? Give us feedback, ideas, or just say hi at walnutpublishing@gmail.com, and if you like Aston Sanderson's writing style, join his email list here: bit.ly/astonsanderson

Printed in Great Britain
by Amazon